WHAT DINOSAURS ATE

For a free color catalog describing Gareth Stevens' list of high-quality books and multimedia programs, call 1-800-542-2595 (USA) or 1-800-461-9120 (Canada). Gareth Stevens Publishing's Fax: (414) 225-0377.

Library of Congress Cataloging-in-Publication Data

Green, Tamara, 1945-
   What dinosaurs ate/by Tamara Green; illustrated by Richard Grant.
     p. cm. — (World of dinosaurs)
   Includes bibliographical references and index.
   Summary: Describes the probable eating habits of various dinosaurs, including carnivores, herbivores, fish-eaters, scavengers, and cannibals, based on the size and shape of their fossilized teeth and the remains found in their stomach cavities.
   ISBN 0-8368-2295-1 (lib. bdg.)
   1. Dinosaurs—Food—Juvenile literature. [1. Dinosaurs—Food. 2. Fossils. 3. Paleontology.] I. Grant, Richard, 1959- ill. II. Title. III. Series: World of dinosaurs.
QE862.D5G73488   1999
567'.9—dc21   98-31769

This North American edition first published in 1999 by
Gareth Stevens Publishing
1555 North RiverCenter Drive, Suite 201
Milwaukee, Wisconsin 53212 USA

This U.S. edition © 1999 by Gareth Stevens, Inc.
Created with original © 1998 by Quartz Editorial Services,
112 Station Road, Edgware HA8 7AQ U.K.
Additional end matter © 1999 by Gareth Stevens, Inc.

Consultant: Dr. Paul Barrett, Paleontologist, Specialist in Biology and
  Evolution of Dinosaurs, University of Cambridge, England.

Printed in Mexico

1 2 3 4 5 6 7 8 9 03 02 01 00 99

WORLD OF DINOSAURS

WHAT DINOSAURS ATE

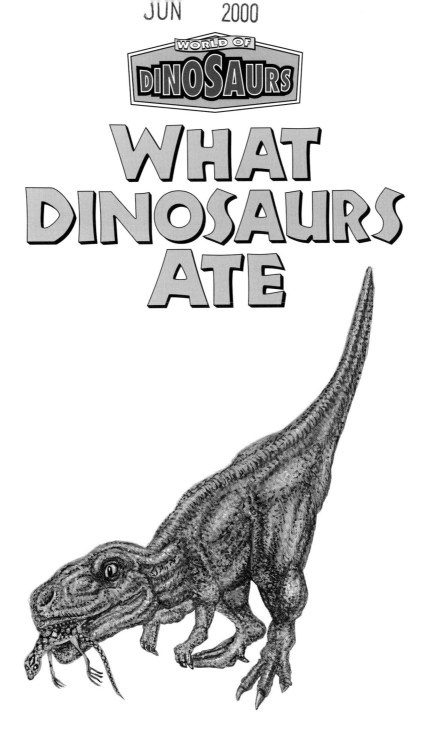

by Tamara Green
Illustrations by Richard Grant

Gareth Stevens Publishing
MILWAUKEE

CONTENTS

INTRODUCTION

What a terrifying sight it must have been when a mighty meat-eater like **Tyrannosaurus rex** went in for the kill. Such carnivorous dinosaurs were always on the prowl for a meal of raw flesh.

Other dinosaurs, however, such as the sauropod *above*, were strict herbivores by nature, obtaining all the nourishment they needed from plants alone. In fact, the larger sauropods would regularly chomp their way through enormous quantities of vegetation.

Some smaller dinosaurs enjoyed snacks of insects from time to time, while others would occasionally feast on eggs. There were meat-eating dinosaurs, too, that would scavenge from any carcass they happened to come

across. And it may, perhaps, come as something of a surprise to learn that there is definite evidence that some dinosaurs were even cannibalistic at times.

How can paleontologists tell which dinosaurs ate which sorts of food? As you will find when you turn the pages that follow, there are several types of clues they can look for — including the size and shape of the teeth, the type of jaw, whether or not they had beaks, actual stomach contents, and fossilized droppings. Read on, and learn about what was on the prehistoric menu.

HUNGRY HERBIVORES

Fossil finds show that most species of dinosaurs were herbivores, eating large amounts of plants, berries, and small fruit.

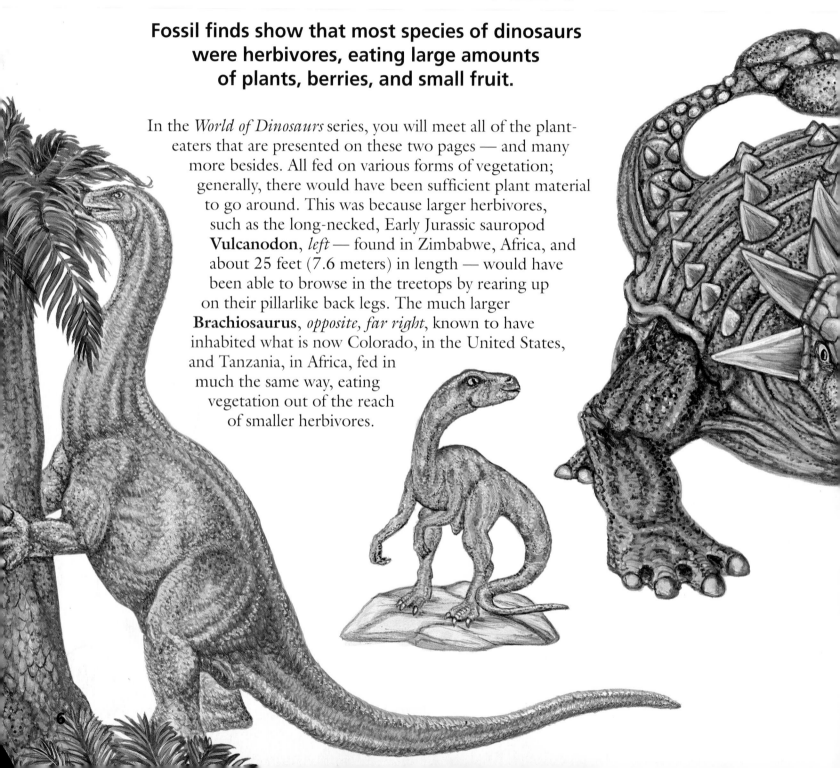

In the *World of Dinosaurs* series, you will meet all of the plant-eaters that are presented on these two pages — and many more besides. All fed on various forms of vegetation; generally, there would have been sufficient plant material to go around. This was because larger herbivores, such as the long-necked, Early Jurassic sauropod **Vulcanodon**, *left* — found in Zimbabwe, Africa, and about 25 feet (7.6 meters) in length — would have been able to browse in the treetops by rearing up on their pillarlike back legs. The much larger **Brachiosaurus**, *opposite, far right*, known to have inhabited what is now Colorado, in the United States, and Tanzania, in Africa, fed in much the same way, eating vegetation out of the reach of smaller herbivores.

6

Bipedal, Triassic **Pisanosaurus**, *opposite, center*, discovered in Argentina, however, was only 3 feet (0.9 m) long and must have fed on ferns and other forms of low-lying vegetation. It therefore did not compete with the sauropods for food.

Heavily armored, 35-foot (10.7-m)-long Cretaceous **Ankylosaurus**, shown *above*, from what is now North America, was sometimes described as a "living tank." It did not attack for food, but took advantage of its bony plates and body spikes to defend itself if a carnivore threatened. Its diet was vegetarian, and it probably fed alongside the giant sauropods, munching its way through great quantities of plant material every day to keep its strength up, given its tremendous size and bulk.

What is now Australia, meanwhile, was home to a smaller plant-eater that was 23 feet (7 m) in length and now known as **Muttaburrasaurus**, *above left*. It was endowed with magnificent thumb spikes, but used these only for self-defense when up against a hungry predator.

When threatened by carnivores, the slight, Triassic **Sellosaurus**, *above right*, another herbivore, also had to rely on its big thumb claws for protection.

Turn now, and find out how these massive plant-eaters managed to digest huge quantities of leaves.

7

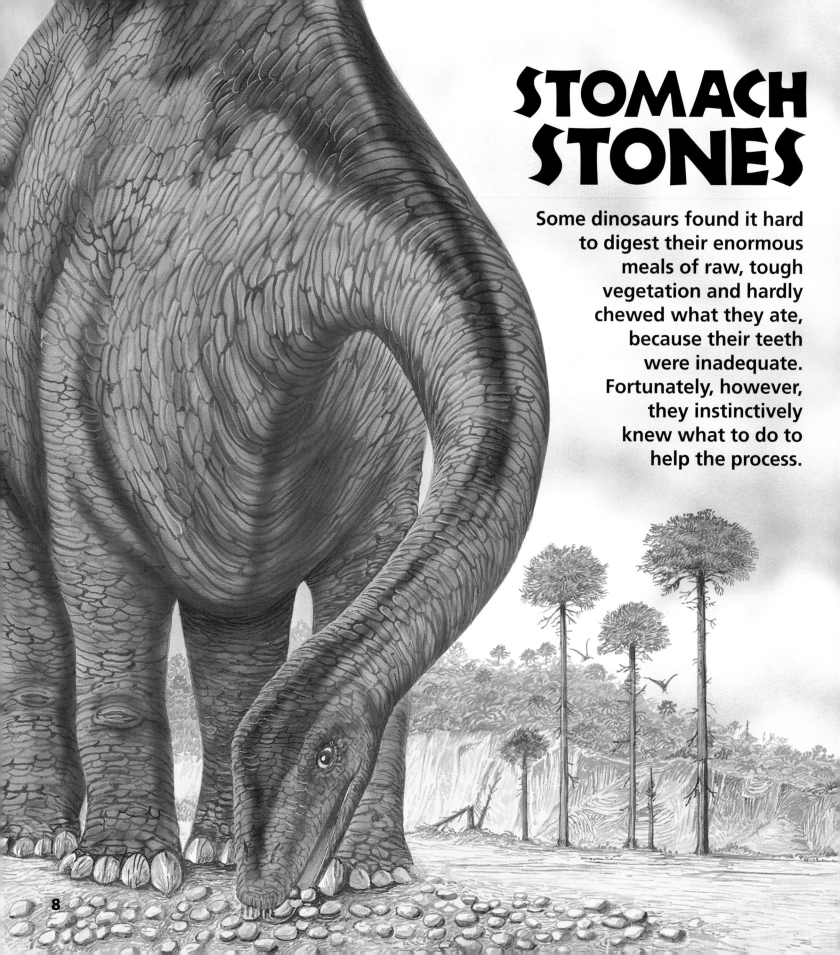

STOMACH STONES

Some dinosaurs found it hard to digest their enormous meals of raw, tough vegetation and hardly chewed what they ate, because their teeth were inadequate. Fortunately, however, they instinctively knew what to do to help the process.

The young sauropod had often watched others in the herd as they fed from lush Jurassic vegetation. It had seen the adult population lapping up cool water from a nearby lake, too, and soon got into this routine as well. At times, the more mature dinosaurs in the herd seemed to do something rather strange, raking up liberal supplies of rough stones in their snouts and then swallowing them in a few quick gulps. As it sniffed a few stones that gleamed in the sunlight, the young sauropod wondered if these could be wholesome and delicious, too. However, they gave out no appetizing aroma and were much too hard to bite.

Nevertheless, the sauropod downed a mouthful. Hungry now for a meal of fresh vegetation, the young creature scampered off to rejoin the herd as they began to tear off large quantities of rubbery leaves for a midday meal.

They all ate greedily — so greedily, in fact, that they did not even attempt to chew their vegetative intake. Painful indigestion would have been inevitable, had it not been for the precautions these herbivores had taken by swallowing lots of stones. Inside the gizzard, these stones would aid digestion by grinding their lunch into a more easily digestible form. The young sauropod had wisely followed suit and, as a result, would not suffer indigestion.

Breaking down

The principal problem for a plant-eating dinosaur was that its food was largely made up of a substance called cellulose. This was, and still is, almost impossible to digest without certain enzymes. Luckily, however, herbivores were, and still are, able to make use of bacteria in their systems that convert the cellulose in their diet into sugars. (Interestingly, some experts believe the human appendix, now a functionless organ, once contributed to our digestion of cellulose.)

In the absence of grinding teeth, sauropods would swallow pebbles, known as gastroliths. Inside their gizzards, the plant material would then be churned around, as it might be by a modern food processor, and would be pulverized by the stones. Eventually, the resulting substance would pass into the dinosaur's intestines so that digestion could be completed and all the valuable nutrients extracted and absorbed.

The skeletal remains of several of the major sauropods have provided evidence that gastroliths were used to aid digestion in this way. Other types of herbivores, however — such as **Iguanodon** — did not need to swallow stones for this purpose. Instead, they could rely on long rows of cheek teeth for adequate chewing. Some herbivores even had cheek pouches where food could be stored for a while prior to digestion. Such pouches may also have prevented food from falling out of their mouths.

Paleontologists have evidence that sauropods were not the only dinosaurs to swallow stones. Many were also found in the stomach region of a **Psittacosaurus** — a dinosaur with a birdlike beak — unearthed in Mongolia. It, too, must have needed help in turning a meal of tough leaves into digestible pulp.

GREEDY CARNIVORES

Meals of insects and lizards may have been sufficient for small carnivores, but larger species needed to hunt for prey that would provide more substantial fare.

Allosaurus, *center of spread*, was a typical carnosaur, measuring 36 feet (11 m) in length with gigantic, powerful jaws that housed lots of sharp, serrated teeth. It was, according to discoveries made to date, the most prolific predator roaming Jurassic North America.

However, not all meat-eaters were as massive as **Allosaurus**. Triassic **Syntarsus**, for instance, *above*, found in Arizona and in Zimbabwe, Africa, was only 10 feet (3 m) long and extremely slender. It probably ate lizards, but may at times have hunted in packs in order to capture a young, small prosauropod. **Ischisaurus**, too, shown *bottom right* on this page, was from Triassic times, and even smaller than **Syntarsus** at just 7 feet (2 m) long. It was one of the earliest carnivorous

dinosaurs and, although it would seem large to us today, was pint-sized in comparison with later monsters.

Some carnivores had specially adapted features that turned them into virtual big-game hunters. **Deinonychus**, *above*, is a prime example. It no doubt used the

10

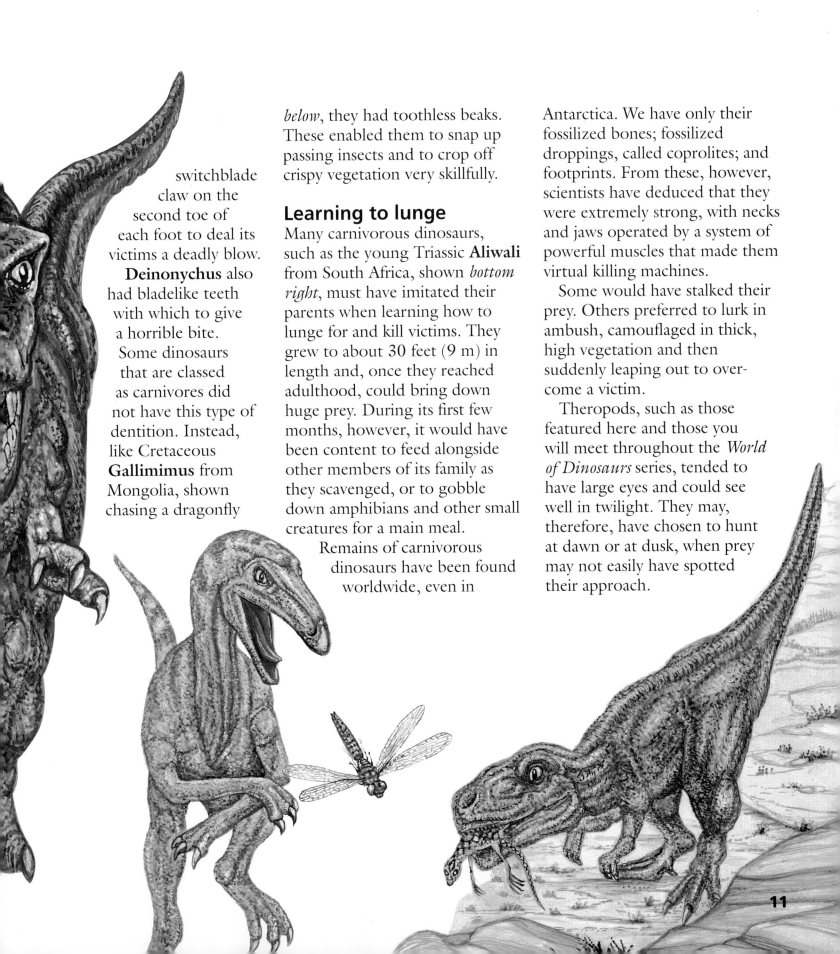

switchblade claw on the second toe of each foot to deal its victims a deadly blow. **Deinonychus** also had bladelike teeth with which to give a horrible bite. Some dinosaurs that are classed as carnivores did not have this type of dentition. Instead, like Cretaceous **Gallimimus** from Mongolia, shown chasing a dragonfly

below, they had toothless beaks. These enabled them to snap up passing insects and to crop off crispy vegetation very skillfully.

Learning to lunge

Many carnivorous dinosaurs, such as the young Triassic **Aliwali** from South Africa, shown *bottom right*, must have imitated their parents when learning how to lunge for and kill victims. They grew to about 30 feet (9 m) in length and, once they reached adulthood, could bring down huge prey. During its first few months, however, it would have been content to feed alongside other members of its family as they scavenged, or to gobble down amphibians and other small creatures for a main meal.

Remains of carnivorous dinosaurs have been found worldwide, even in Antarctica. We have only their fossilized bones; fossilized droppings, called coprolites; and footprints. From these, however, scientists have deduced that they were extremely strong, with necks and jaws operated by a system of powerful muscles that made them virtual killing machines.

Some would have stalked their prey. Others preferred to lurk in ambush, camouflaged in thick, high vegetation and then suddenly leaping out to overcome a victim.

Theropods, such as those featured here and those you will meet throughout the *World of Dinosaurs* series, tended to have large eyes and could see well in twilight. They may, therefore, have chosen to hunt at dawn or at dusk, when prey may not easily have spotted their approach.

11

OUT FOR THE KILL!

Scientists believe some dinosaurs hunted in packs in order to capture larger prey. The massive meal could then be shared.

The chase was on, as three ravenous **Deinonychus**, slim-bodied and built for speed, raced after the timid, young **Tenontosaurus**. The much-larger prey was a gentle dinosaur that, like **Deinonychus,** roamed the open plains of Oklahoma in Early Cretaceous times.

As a rule, the herbivore would have stayed close to the rest of the herd into which it had been born. On this particular day, however, it had shown a spirit of adventure and gone off to explore a little on its own. Such a rare display of independence was to prove unwise. Little did it know that a marauding pack of sickle-clawed hunters was near at hand. There would be little chance of survival.

Deinonychus belonged to a group of dinosaurs called dromaeosaurids, which also included **Dromaeosaurus** and **Velociraptor**. This bipedal flesh-eater was among the fastest of all the dinosaurs.

Theropod thugs

Up to 11 feet (3.3 m) in length and with sharp, bladelike teeth, **Deinonychus** nevertheless relied most heavily on its mighty switchblade claws — one on each foot. These could be flicked forward time and again to deliver a whole series of nasty slashes.

When out for the kill, a group of several of these hungry carnivores would lurk in a rocky or forested area, waiting for a suitable opportunity. Then, together, they would run down and surround their prey, jumping onto the victim's back. Next, each would use one of its switchblade claws to cling to the poor creature. With its other mighty foot claw, each would tear open the victim's flesh. Shock and injury usually meant that death came rapidly. But a pack was sometimes so greedy that its members may

have fed while the victim was still writhing in agony and struggling to survive.

Hunting in packs certainly had its advantages — all the more so for smaller predators lacking these formidable claws. In fact, it is possible that a small group of carnivores such as **Coelurus,**

each 6 feet (1.8 m) long, would have been able to overcome a lone **Diplodocus** that weighed 12 tons and was 87 feet (26.5 m) long if the circumstances were right. Most probably, the pack would have tried to get the sauropod onto its side.

This would have kept it from getting up and attempting to defend itself by kicking out with its stocky feet and lashing its whiplike tail.

Sometimes, packs were even larger, as paleontologists have discovered from fossilized tracks located in Bolivia, South America. These show that, in Jurassic times, a herd of sauropods was once chased by as many as fifty carnivores. What a sight that must have been!

EGG-THIEVES

Some dinosaurs, such as Oviraptor in the Cretaceous period, probably enjoyed feasting on eggs, so the developing babies inside would often have been at risk.

The mother **Pteranodon** had been sitting on her eggs for several hours and was beginning to feel hungry. Responding to her nagging appetite, she flew down from the cliff and swooped to catch a meal of fish. It was delicious; but this pterosaur parent would soon squawk with rage and distress when she returned to find that there were now just two eggs on the cliff edge. Only a few minutes before, there had been three. What sort of creature could have robbed her nest?

Fresh tracks provided a sure sign that a predatory dinosaur had been on the prowl. The developing baby inside the egg had probably stood no chance. The egg had been snatched up in powerful jaws, the hungry dinosaur biting into it and sucking out the rich contents. Several unpalatable shards of broken shell were not swallowed, but spit out and left as evidence.

From now on, the mother would have to keep a closer eye on her offspring. Once a dinosaur that was partial to eggs knew where some could be found, it might try its luck again, with equally disastrous results for an unborn pterosaur.

It is likely that some species of dinosaurs regularly went out of their way to steal eggs, if a more substantial meal was not available. This was, in fact, how the Cretaceous, birdlike dinosaur **Oviraptor** came to be called by a name meaning "egg-thief." It was first discovered in Mongolia's Gobi Desert during the 1920s, near a clutch of eggs thought to have been laid by the plant-eater **Protoceratops**.

Defending the nest

Scientists first assumed that beaked **Oviraptor** had died while raiding the nest for a meal of newly laid eggs, which it could easily crack open with its two-pronged upper jaws. The current view, however, rejects this theory, since study of the bones of the nearby unhatched embryos has shown that these eggs may have actually belonged to the **Oviraptor** itself. **Oviraptor**, at least on this occasion, may not have been the thief but most probably a caring parent that had died defending its brood. Which other creature in the prehistoric landscape, then, could have been the culprit?

It is unlikely to have been a **Protoceratops**, since this particular dinosaur was strictly an herbivore. Maybe a rival **Oviraptor** was to blame or, more likely, a pack of **Velociraptor**. These swift hunters, also from Cretaceous times, were small and slender, and their skeletons have been discovered in the same region of Mongolia. Certainly, there are fossilized remains that show **Velociraptor** grappling to overcome a **Protoceratops**. So it may have fought with an **Oviraptor**, too, over a clutch of eggs.

Eggs would usually be covered with layers of dried vegetation,

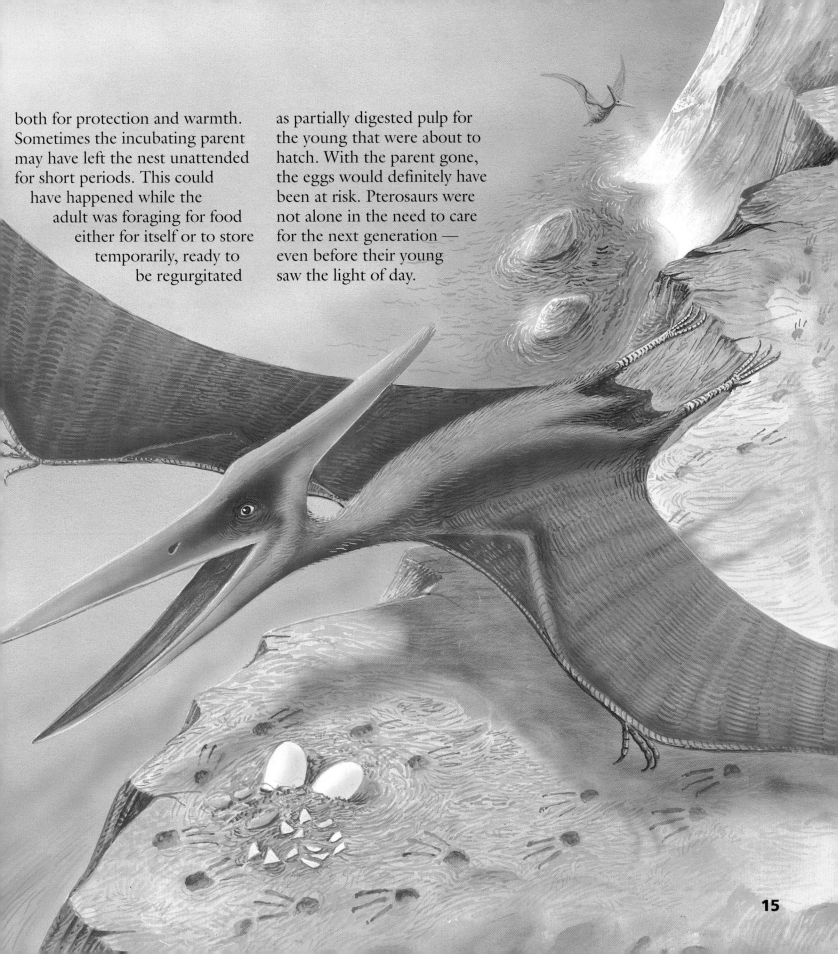

both for protection and warmth. Sometimes the incubating parent may have left the nest unattended for short periods. This could have happened while the adult was foraging for food either for itself or to store temporarily, ready to be regurgitated as partially digested pulp for the young that were about to hatch. With the parent gone, the eggs would definitely have been at risk. Pterosaurs were not alone in the need to care for the next generation — even before their young saw the light of day.

MEALS

Roses
Flowering plants first evolved during Cretaceous times. Among them were **roses**, much like those we know today, and also magnolias. Herbivores that fed on low-lying vegetation may have enjoyed such delicately perfumed additions to their daily plant intake.

Classopolis
Sauropods would have found it easy to browse on Jurassic **Classopolis**, a **conifer** that grew to 40 feet (12 m) in height. Paleobotanists have even succeeded in isolating pollen from its fossils.

OF PLANTS

Ginkgoes
Also known as maidenhairs, **ginkgoes** were widespread as early as Triassic times and are still planted today as ornamental trees. Herbivores would have found their distinctive fan-shaped leaves easy to digest.

Conifers
Several types of **conifers** probably flourished throughout the time dinosaurs roamed our planet. Some still exist today, many millions of years later.

Cycads
These pineapple-shaped plants were a common feature of the dinosaurs' landscape. **Cycads** had palmlike fans of leaves that sprouted from the top of their tough, scaly, bulbous bases. Plant-eating dinosaurs would have found such leaves delicious.

DINOSAUR

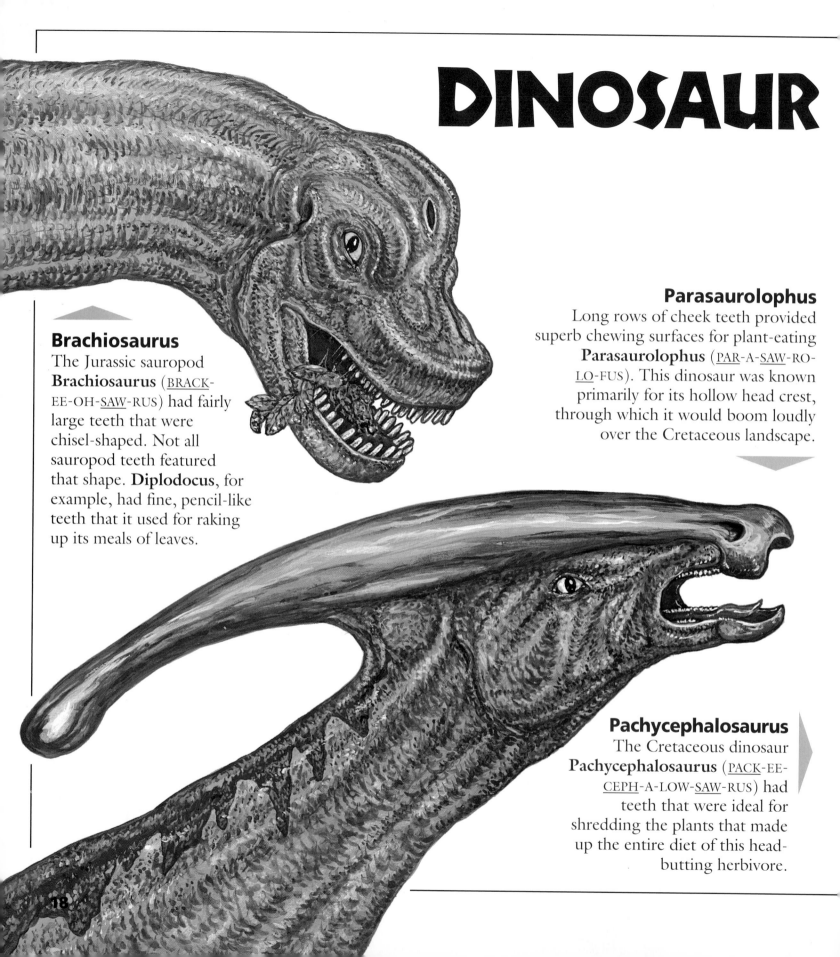

Brachiosaurus
The Jurassic sauropod **Brachiosaurus** (<u>BRACK</u>-EE-OH-<u>SAW</u>-RUS) had fairly large teeth that were chisel-shaped. Not all sauropod teeth featured that shape. **Diplodocus**, for example, had fine, pencil-like teeth that it used for raking up its meals of leaves.

Parasaurolophus
Long rows of cheek teeth provided superb chewing surfaces for plant-eating **Parasaurolophus** (<u>PAR</u>-A-<u>SAW</u>-RO-<u>LO</u>-FUS). This dinosaur was known primarily for its hollow head crest, through which it would boom loudly over the Cretaceous landscape.

Pachycephalosaurus
The Cretaceous dinosaur **Pachycephalosaurus** (<u>PACK</u>-EE-<u>CEPH</u>-A-LOW-<u>SAW</u>-RUS) had teeth that were ideal for shredding the plants that made up the entire diet of this head-butting herbivore.

TEETH-1

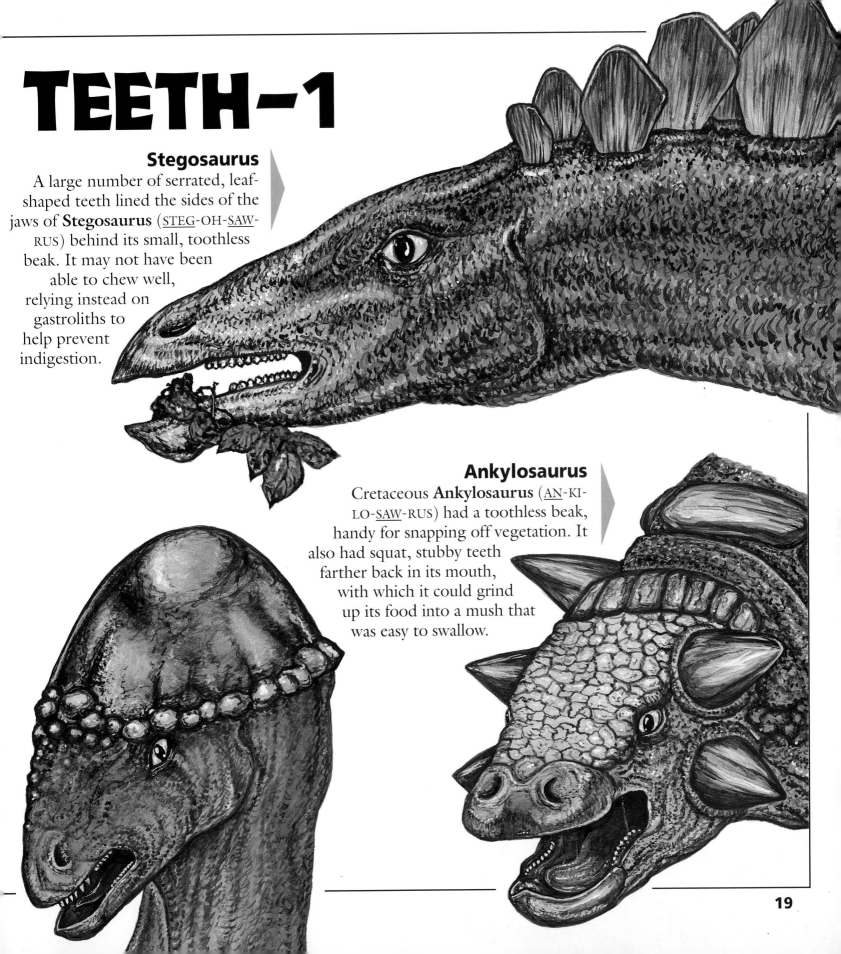

Stegosaurus

A large number of serrated, leaf-shaped teeth lined the sides of the jaws of **Stegosaurus** (STEG-OH-SAW-RUS) behind its small, toothless beak. It may not have been able to chew well, relying instead on gastroliths to help prevent indigestion.

Ankylosaurus

Cretaceous **Ankylosaurus** (AN-KI-LO-SAW-RUS) had a toothless beak, handy for snapping off vegetation. It also had squat, stubby teeth farther back in its mouth, with which it could grind up its food into a mush that was easy to swallow.

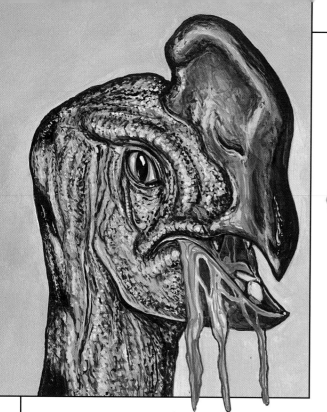

DINOSAUR

Oviraptor

Crested, birdlike **Oviraptor** (OV-EE-RAP-TOR) was toothless, but had powerful, two-pronged jaws behind its short, sharp beak. Some experts believe this beak may have been particularly well-suited for cracking open a meal of eggs or for biting off vegetation. The prongs were set in the roof of its mouth.

Tyrannosaurus rex

Like all large carnivores, Cretaceous **Tyrannosaurus rex** (TIE-RAN-OH-SAW-RUS RECKS) had huge, razor-sharp teeth that pointed backward, very effective for grasping struggling prey. These giant meat-eaters did not chew. Instead, they swallowed large chunks of raw flesh whole.

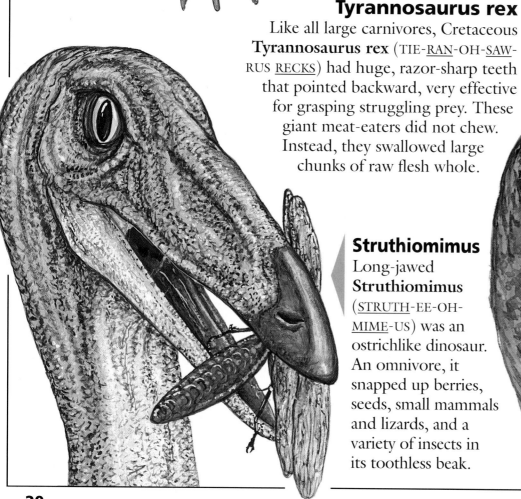

Struthiomimus

Long-jawed **Struthiomimus** (STRUTH-EE-OH-MIME-US) was an ostrichlike dinosaur. An omnivore, it snapped up berries, seeds, small mammals and lizards, and a variety of insects in its toothless beak.

20

TEETH-2

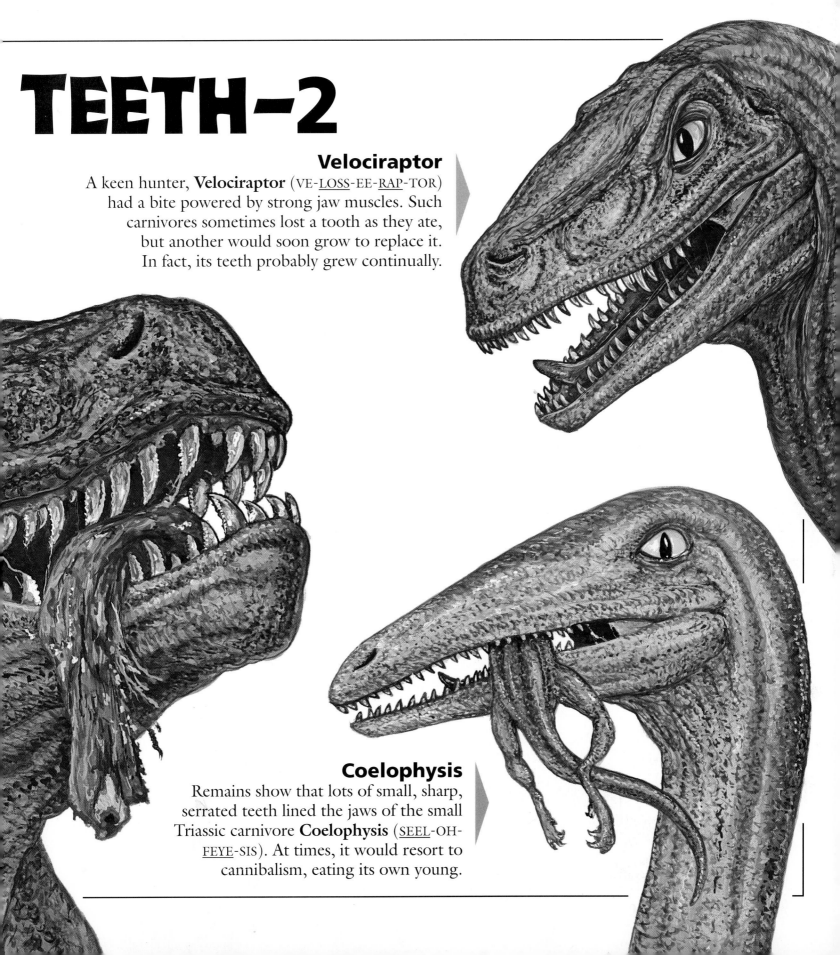

Velociraptor

A keen hunter, **Velociraptor** (VE-LOSS-EE-RAP-TOR) had a bite powered by strong jaw muscles. Such carnivores sometimes lost a tooth as they ate, but another would soon grow to replace it. In fact, its teeth probably grew continually.

Coelophysis

Remains show that lots of small, sharp, serrated teeth lined the jaws of the small Triassic carnivore **Coelophysis** (SEEL-OH-FEYE-SIS). At times, it would resort to cannibalism, eating its own young.

SCAVENGING

Sometimes a dinosaur would die of natural causes, or perhaps a large carnivore would not entirely devour its prey. Then it was time for scavengers to step in.

The bipedal flesh-eater and its offspring were excited. The **Coelurus** had not eaten yet that day and were feeling sharp hunger pangs. They had just spotted the carcass of a young, plant-eating **Stegosaurus** lying on the sandy ground below.

Some mighty predator, or perhaps a pack of smaller meat-eaters, must have killed it earlier in the morning and feasted on its flesh.

Its ribs were now almost entirely exposed, and the upright bony plates that had once lined its back, offering a built-in means of temperature control, were almost buried in the sand.

The **Coelurus**, however, were going to be disappointed. All of the meat had been eaten, and there was nothing to salvage. They were often more fortunate, however, and benefited from the leftovers of bigger, more powerful

carnivores to supplement their diet of smaller prey.

Some large carnivores may have scavenged in addition to hunting because they were not always successful at gaining ground on their prey. Or, they may not have been able to obtain adequate nourishment from their prey if it was a very small species, so they occasionally resorted to scavenging to increase the amount of meat they consumed.

Daily requirements

How much did a carnivore actually need to eat? One dinosaurologist has calculated that **Ornitholestes**, weighing about 28 pounds (13 kilograms), probably needed to eat about 1.5 pounds (0.7 kg) of flesh every day — the equivalent of six quarter-pound (0.1 kg) hamburgers. A carnivore as large as a 7-ton **Tyrannosaurus rex**, however, might have needed to feast on as much as 200 pounds (91 kg) of meat daily, or even more, simply in order to survive. If the carnivore could not find adequate food through hunting, however, it would have turned to scavenging. It may even have resorted to stealing the prey of smaller carnivores.

On the other hand, if it had a successful hunt and overcame a 5-ton **Triceratops**, it would have been satisfied long before all of its prey had been consumed. The carcass would then provide a meal for other hungry, passing scavengers once the killer had moved on.

In the heat of a prehistoric day, there was always the risk that uneaten flesh could turn putrid, or that flies and other insects would land on the carcass and spread disease. As a result, scavengers ran the risk of becoming ill if they ate scraps of meat that had been lying around for days.

Experts have evidence that some dinosaurs — such as Triassic **Coelophysis** — ate their young at times; in this respect, they could be described as cannibals. Fossilized stomach contents unearthed by scientists have shown this to be the case. At first, experts thought the skeletal remains of the babies were actually developing embryos. However, scientists have now discovered that dinosaurs did not give birth to live young, but laid eggs from which their offspring hatched.

We will probably never know for certain whether these babies were eaten when still alive or swallowed after having been killed. It is possible that the mother **Coelophysis** ate her young in a desperate but tragic attempt to protect them from other predators. Whatever the case, carnivorous dinosaurs were certainly bloodthirsty beasts.

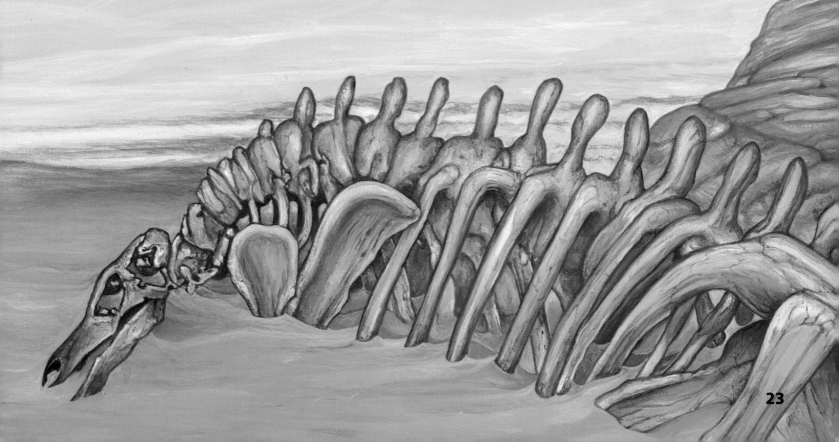

FISHING FOR FOOD

Fossilized stomach contents point to the fact that at least one species of dinosaur hunted near prehistoric seas, rivers, and lakes, gobbling up live fish to satisfy a voracious appetite.

A warm Cretaceous morning had just dawned, and two dinosaurs of the **Baryonyx** species had ambled down to the water's edge. What more pleasant way could there have been to start the prehistoric day than to slurp down a cool, refreshing drink! From their experience, the pair also knew that there were abundant supplies of marine life in this particular coastal area, and that a little patience would be rewarded with tasty fish.

Huge sea creatures also would occasionally approach the shore — massively jawed mosasaurs, for instance, that might try to attack a browsing **Baryonyx** if extremely hungry and given half a chance. Dolphinlike ichthyosaurs, long-necked plesiosaurs, and predatory pliosaurs also sometimes swam toward shore. Pterosaurs, too, would frequently swoop down from the skies to catch a meal of fish that happened to be near the surface. The two **Baryonx** would have to be quick if they were to

feed and also escape becoming breakfast themselves for some marauding marine monster.

Fortunately, they were lucky this particular morning. Almost simultaneously, both became aware of a flurry beneath the surf. Using their mighty thumb claws, each snatched up an unsuspecting, sizable fish that had been swimming in the shallows. Speedily, both downed the slippery prey in a single gulp, bones and all, not bothering to chew and savor the tasty flesh. **Baryonyx** was a large beast with a hearty appetite, and it would not stop fishing until it felt entirely satisfied.

Scientists are certain that **Baryonyx** ate fish either as its staple diet or, at least, from time to time. Proof is offered by the undigested fish scales that have been found in its remains. The victim has even been identified as **Lepidotes**, which grew to 3 feet (0.9 m) in length. This provided a fairly substantial snack of fish for

Baryonyx, a theropod that weighed 2 tons and reached 30 feet (9 m) in length.

Built-in weapons

Baryonyx certainly seems to have lived up to its name, which means "heavy claw." In fact, its powerful thumb weapons were 12 inches (30 centimeters) long and very sharp.

At times, **Baryonyx** may have waded out quite a distance in pursuit of a marine victim, in spite of the risks involved. It is likely to have hunted land-based prey as well, and may also have scavenged.

The first part of **Baryonyx**'s remains to be discovered was one of its thumb claws. Unearthed by an amateur fossil collector, it was found next to the remains of an **Iguanodon**. This herbivore also had thumb weapons, and the two may have engaged in combat. Fish, it seems, on the whole, would have provided a much more readily accessible and equally nutritious food source.

ON THE MOVE

Sauropods regularly ate enormous amounts of vegetation, rapidly stripping the foliage from vast areas of forest. Each herbivore needed a lot of nourishment to energize a huge, bulky frame, and a large supply of water to quench a giant thirst. No wonder large herds frequently migrated in search of new feeding grounds.

For the moment, the herd of giant sauropods felt full and somewhat lethargic. In just a few hours, though, these large, long-necked creatures would move on as hunger set in again. For animals with such large appetites, it was vital to find fresh food supplies in forested areas that had not recently been stripped by other herds of herbivores.

Tracks of migrating dinosaurs that were searching for food have been located worldwide —

in places as far apart as Asia, Europe, and Africa, as well as North and South America. Some of the most spectacular tracks have been found in Texas, in the United States. Much has been learned about the behavior of the dinosaurs that left these prints million of years ago.

Young and tender

Experts have been able to determine, for instance, that, when dinosaurs migrated in this way, they often shepherded their young to the center of the herd. Many animals still do this today, so that the young are well protected from attack. With a keen sense of smell, a carnivore could easily sniff out tempting prey from a distance. Without protection from the adults, the young would have been very

vulnerable, and it would have been more difficult for them to escape attackers and defend themselves.

Scientists have even identified the tracks of three carnosaurs as they converged with those of twelve sauropods. One sauropod footprint is clearly missing where the tracks meet — a sign, some paleontologists believe, that the carnivores probably attacked one of the sauropods at that exact location.

Some carnivores may have been intelligent enough to locate prey simply by following fresh sauropod tracks. The skeletons of many of these dinosaurs disintegrated long ago, but evidence of their migration remains in the form of footprints and coprolites. These are known as trace fossils.

FATAL FAMINE

A number of theories still exist as to why dinosaurs became extinct about 65 million years ago, among them the possibility that food suddenly got scarce or even disappeared altogether.

As the ground shook all over planet Earth, whole herds of terrified dinosaurs — herbivores and carnivores alike — stood rooted to the spot in panic. Large chunks of rock were suddenly thrown up into the air, and thick clouds of dust soon made it difficult to breathe.

Throughout the major landmasses, the largest of the meat-eaters reared up and roared as if in self-defense. Smaller species, together with plant-eaters of all sizes, quivered and cowered, too shocked to bellow loud warnings to their fellow creatures. It was almost as if the whole world was on the point of exploding.

Within just a few hours, complete devastation had occurred. Thousands of dinosaurs lay writhing in agony on the ground, unable to rise to their feet. Even those that had so far managed to escape affliction were to perish before too long. These were Late Cretaceous times, and the period of 163 million years during which dinosaurs had ruled supreme was soon to be dramatically curtailed.

Beginning of the end

People still wonder why dinosaurs became extinct. Most scientists agree, however, with the American scientists Luis and Walter Alvarez, who said that an astonishingly large, red-hot asteroid from somewhere in outer space collided with our planet. Up to 6 miles (9.6 kilometers) wide and traveling at 60,000 miles (96,500 km) per hour, it would have penetrated deep into Earth's crust. The evidence is a massive crater in Mexico and the presence of the mineral iridium, a substance not usually found on Earth but nevertheless located and identified by this father-and-son team in Late Cretaceous deposits.

Earthquakes and giant tidal waves are said to have resulted from the collision on a worldwide scale. Sunlight was gradually obliterated, and the world was plunged into darkness. Huge changes in climatic conditions occurred, too. Photosynthesis, for which light is essential, could no longer take place. Plant life, therefore, failed to flourish, and terrible famine resulted as part of this major global catastrophe.

Herbivores went hungry and may have died both as a result of inhalation of the polluted atmosphere and sheer physical weakness. Meanwhile, the carnivores that had the strength to scavenge on the herbivores' remains may have unknowingly eaten poisoned flesh.

What remains a complete mystery, however, is how some life-forms, including the small mammals and birds that had already started to evolve, managed to survive this cataclysmic event. This puzzle continues to perplex leading paleontologists to this day.

GLOSSARY

appendix — a slender tube attached to the large intestine.

asteroid — one of the thousands of small planets, especially between Mars and Jupiter, that orbit the Sun.

bipedal — relating to an animal that walks or moves on two feet.

browse — to feed on the tender shoots, twigs, and leaves of trees and shrubs.

cannibal — an animal that feeds on others of its own kind.

carcass — the body of a dead animal; a corpse.

carnivorous — relating to a meat-eating animal.

cellulose — a substance found in plants that is hard to digest.

clutch (n) — a nest of eggs; a brood, or group, of young recently hatched from eggs.

coprolites — fossilized dung, or animal droppings.

Cretaceous times — the final era of the dinosaurs, lasting from 144-65 million years ago.

cycads — pineapple-shaped plants with fans of leaves sprouting from the top of a tough, bulblike base.

dentition — the number and arrangement of teeth within an animal's mouth.

digest — to break food down into a form that can be absorbed and used by the body.

enzymes — substances produced by the body that aid digestion.

foraging — wandering or roaming in search of food; feeding by grazing or browsing.

fossilized — embedded and preserved in rocks, resin, or other material.

gastroliths — small stones swallowed by some plant-eating dinosaurs to help with the digestion of tough plant material.

gizzard — a part of the stomach area of some animals that has a thick, muscular wall and a tough lining for grinding food.

ichthyosaurs — extinct marine reptiles that had fishlike bodies and long snouts.

instinctively — behaving in a way that is natural, or automatic, rather than learned.

Jurassic times — the middle era of the dinosaurs, lasting from 213-144 million years ago.

omnivore — an animal that eats both plants and meat.

paleobotanist — a scientist who studies the fossilized remains of plants.

paleontologist — a scientist who studies past geologic periods as they are known from fossil remains.

prolific — producing young or fruit in great numbers.

prosauropod — any member of a group of moderately long-necked dinosaurs, all herbivores, mainly from Triassic times.

pulverized — crushed or ground into a powder or tiny particles.

sauropod — a plant-eating, long-necked dinosaur, mainly from Jurassic times, that had a small head and five-toed feet.

scavenge — to eat the leftovers or carcasses of other animals.

theropods — members of a group of carnivorous, bipedal dinosaurs.

trace fossils — remains, such as tracks or droppings, that can be studied to learn more about prehistoric animal life.

Triassic times — the first era of the dinosaurs, lasting from 249-213 million years ago.

MORE BOOKS TO READ

The Best Book of Dinosaurs. Christopher Maynard (Kingfisher)

Death from Space: What Killed the Dinosaurs? Isaac Asimov and Greg Walz-Chojnacki (Gareth Stevens)

Dinosaur Dinners. Sharon Cosner (Franklin Watts)

Dinosaurs. Neil Clark (Dorling Kindersley)

Dinosaurs. David Norman (Knopf)

Dinosaurs and How They Lived. Steve Parker (Dorling Kindersley)

How Did Dinosaurs Live? Kunihiko Hisa (Lerner)

Hungry Dinosaurs. Alvin Granowsky (Steck-Vaughn)

The Magic School Bus: In the Time of the Dinosaurs. Joanna Cole (Scholastic)

The New Dinosaur Collection (series). (Gareth Stevens)

Plant-Eating Dinosaurs. David Weishampel (Franklin Watts)

World of Dinosaurs (series). (Gareth Stevens)

VIDEOS

All About Dinosaurs. (United Learning)

Did Comets Kill The Dinosaurs? (Gareth Stevens)

Dinosaur! (series). (Arts & Entertainment Network)

Dinosaurs. (DeBeck Educational Video)

Dinosaurs. (Smithsonian Video)

Dinosaurs, Dinosaurs, Dinosaurs. (Twin Tower Enterprises)

Dinosaurs: The Terrible Lizards. (AIMS Media)

Learning About Dinosaurs. (Trans-Atlantic Video)

The Nature of the Beast. (PBS Video)

WEB SITES

www.clpgh.org/cmnh/discovery/

www.dinodon.com/index.html

www.dinosauria.com/

www.id.iit.edu/~doe/alphadmo_07a/dinosaur.html

www.oink.demon.co.uk/topics/dinosaur.htm

www.ZoomDinosaurs.com

Due to the dynamic nature of the Internet, some web sites stay current longer than others. To find additional web sites, use a reliable search engine with one or more of the following keywords to help you locate more information about dinosaurs. Keywords: *Cretaceous, dinosaurs, fossils, paleobotany, paleontology, prehistoric.*

INDEX